Making the Most of ALL NINE LIVES

The Extraordinary Life of
Buffy the Cat

Sandy Robins and Paul Smulson

TRIUMPH
BOOKS

This book is available in quantity at special discounts for your group or organization. For further information, contact:

    Triumph Books LLC
    814 North Franklin Street
    Chicago, Illinois 60610
    (312) 337-0747
    www.triumphbooks.com

Printed in U.S.A.
ISBN: 978-1-62937-163-4
Design by Patricia Frey
Photography by Paul Smulson

Dedication

To Buffy and orange tabbies everywhere.
Okay, and grey tabbies too.
Scratch that.
To Buffy and ALL cats everywhere...

Acknowledgments

Thank you to Mitch Rogatz and Michelle Bruton at Triumph Books and the wonderful Erin Niumata of the Folio Literary Agency for making this book happen. Also to Alice Smulson, Buffy's personal seamstress along with Bruce Rich, Robin Smulson, and Mike Sandler for their invaluable creative input and support.

Introduction

My first thought, after giggling over a collection of photographs of Buffy the Cat playing golf, perfecting his karate chop, going fishing with the boys, flying a plane, and going on a drug bust with the Chicago police, is that my cats would never allow me to take them places. Further, they won't play dress-up, let alone hold a pose for more than two seconds. Unthinkable! This is probably true for most members of the Felis Catus family....

And that's what makes Buffy so extraordinary—a one-in-a-million cat.

Making the Most of All Nine Lives: The Extraordinary Life of Buffy the Cat highlights some of the special moments when Buffy's dad, photographer Paul Smulson, brought out his camera and captured the very unique human side of Buffy's personality. His expressions instinctively capture the action on hand. Nobody taught him or coaxed him, and there's no trick photography involved. Perhaps it can be put down to trust and an unbreakable, special bond between one man and his orange tabby.

Where do I come in? Well, after a lifetime of loving, rescuing, writing about, and educating the public about felines, my publisher believes I speak "catlish" fluently. So I was hired as Buffy's human translator to put his thoughts behind his actions into words so that cat lovers everywhere can live vicariously, enjoying this amazing feline's people skills and escapades.

Paul, thank you for this once-in-a-lifetime opportunity. I've never had so much fun.

—Sandy Robins

I have a confession: I spent most of my life feeling ambivalent toward cats.

When our neighbor's cat had kittens, my wife Robin and I found ourselves adopting two of them. We named them Buffy and Smokey. How could I refuse? Robin, who never had pets growing up, stated that our daughters would love the cats and, indeed, they did. But I was the one who discovered that there was a besotted cat person hidden inside of me.

I quickly learned how funny cats could be with their playful antics. One day, I put headphones on Buffy and reached for my camera. He sat for five minutes, holding different poses while I snapped away. This was the first of many fun photo sessions that followed. And when I showed the photographs to others, the collective reaction was, "My cat would never do that!" This simply endorsed their universal appeal. Even now, I am unable to determine who was having more fun during the photo sessions featured in this book, Buffy or me.

Thank you Sandy for your passion and expertise and for "voicing" Buffy's thoughts in these captured moments.

From my own personal transformation into a cat lover, I learned that I was not unique. Many people don't realize they are cat lovers until they get an opportunity to interact with a cat. My hope is that by enjoying this book, more people will give cats a chance so that ultimately more deserving felines find love and forever homes.

—Paul Smulson

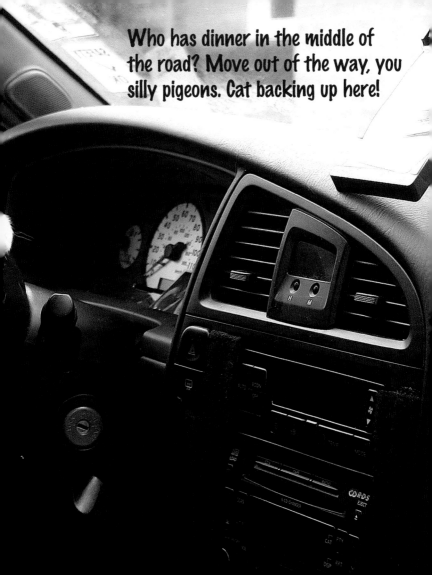

Who has dinner in the middle of the road? Move out of the way, you silly pigeons. Cat backing up here!

Yikes. Gas prices are up again.

Oh well, I have no choice but to fill up.
But my next car will definitely be a hybrid.

Don't wait up. I'm going out for a night on the town.

So a goat fell off a truck and wandered into a bar. This isn't a joke. I kid you not...that's how Chicago's Billy Goat Tavern got its name.

Cheers! I love the way the froth tickles my nose.

Oh dear. I guess...burp...I chased the froth to the bottom of the glassh. Burp. I think that qualifies asshh one too many....

Getting through security
was a breeze...

...where do we go from here?

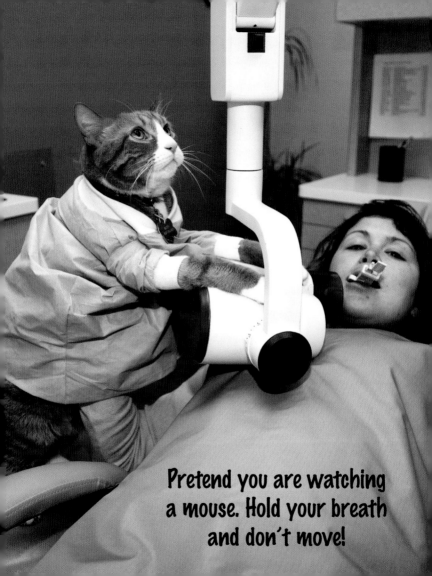

Pretend you are watching
a mouse. Hold your breath
and don't move!

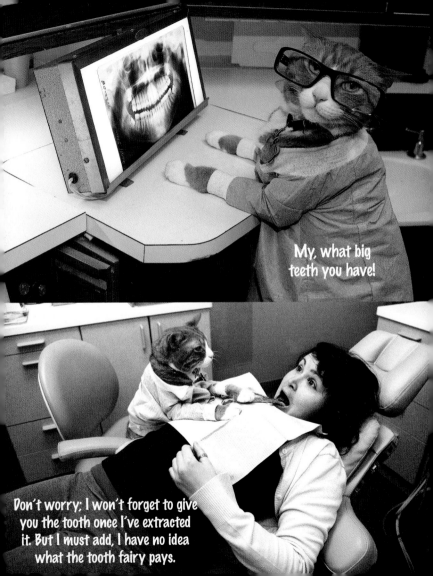

This undercover surveillance work taps directly into my innate feline curiosity.

Clearly their tactics aren't working. Perhaps if I caterwaul and create a ruckus, they will simply open the door.

Good evening and thank you for watching. This is the late edition of the evening news and I'm Buffy the Cat.

Now listen up, kid. I'm going
to teach you how to copycat.

Watch closely. I've got this
pulling-a-rabbit-out-of-a-hat
trick down pat.
Abracadabra... mumbo jumbo....

Any cat that has sat waiting for a mouse to emerge from a hole knows that patience is always rewarded. So checkers is nothing more than a cat and mouse game.

When it comes to playing solitaire, it's all about repeating patterns. Actually, this is a hunting strategy that cats have used for 10,000 years.

Where does it say lick it and stick it?

Okay. So let's get right down to the nuts and bolts of this project.

One of life's
lessons: never
let grass grow
under your feet.

By trimming this hedge I am broadening my horizons. Well, that's what the humans think. Actually, I'm keeping an eye on the neighbor's cute tabby.

There are plusses and minuses for everything. When it snows, shoveling is a real drag.

On the plus side,
I get to make
a new friend.

They say a
watched kettle
never boils.
But eggs are
obviously a
different kettle
of fish...I think
I'm mixing my
metaphors!

Entertaining can be fun. But it's much easier to serve kibble.

Okay,
I've got this.

Nearly there...

Like I said, I've got this....

ICE CREAM ★ & ★ COLD DRINKS ★

Where are the kids today?
Maybe I should ring the bell.
If they don't show soon, I
may be tempted to taste
some of the ice cream.

There is nothing like a little R and R in the middle of the day. But right now I could do with some P and S—push to swing.

Perhaps I should try
this on my back.

CHP stands for Cat Highway Patrol.

Honesty is the best policy. I'm going to tell the teacher the dog ate my homework.

I am officially the Teacher's Pet.

says here that a single variable calculus can deal with the motion of an object ng a fixed path. Hopefully, this will answer how I access that bag of kibble on e top shelf and determine its trajectory to the floor so that I can help myself.

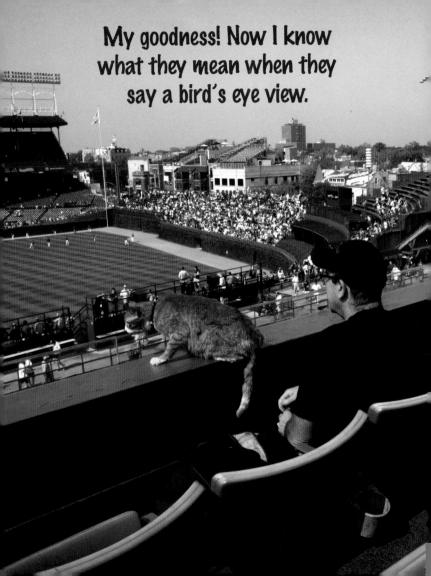

My goodness! Now I know what they mean when they say a bird's eye view.

"LET ME HEAR 'YA ...
A ONE ... A TWO . A THREE ..."

- HARRY CARAY

Holy cow!
It's Harry Caray.

An orange cat BBQ-ing red fish
at a tailgating party. Life is good.

Hey Chicago bear. The fight song
says "Bear Down". So move it!

Ping-pong gives me an opportunity to hone my pounce and prey skills and teaches me to focus on my quarry.

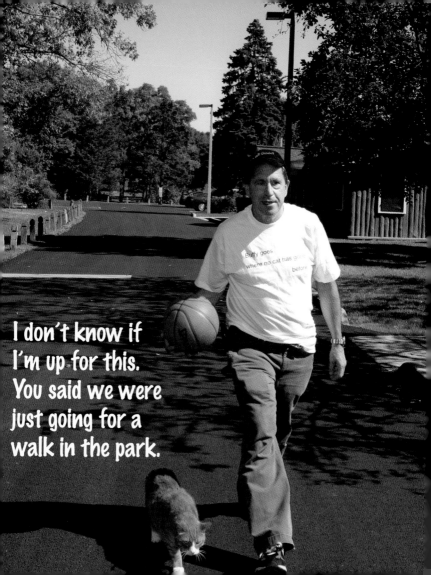

Skateboarding is really fun. Now, if I can figure out how to ollie, I'll be stoked!

As a member of the Felis Catus family, I'm renowned for my agility and flexibility. But even I like to stretch and limber up before a game of golf.

→ 10 Tee
→ Grill Pickup
→ Washrooms
← 1 Tee
← Practice Range

Decisions, decisions. To tee or not to tee? Perhaps heading to the grill is a better idea.

Is this what they mean when they say it's a long shot?

I have this pegged as a birdie of the non-feathered kind.

This Hobie must be one helluva cool cat to have a boat named after him. But since I'm at the helm, I think Buffy's Boat sounds much better.

You said there are lots of fish in the sea. So what's the plan?

Okay boys. The
first catch of
the day is mine.

Hi-yah!! I know, this is not a typical feline sound but meow doesn't quite have the same impact.

Don't underestimate my soft furry paws. A good karate chop is actually a calculated feline kill-skill. Ask any mouse that lived to tell the tale.

When you said you were going to show me the ropes, I thought you meant something else.

They say every vote matters. However, in my house, my vote is the only one that counts!

I think I'm going to valet park.

Wow Buffy! This is a feast—smoked herring and smoked salmon. They are also Paul's favorites. I think we should ask for a doggie, er, kitty bag and take him leftovers.

Smokey: "Buffy, I told you the word you are looking for is kibble. This says kibitz, which means giving unwanted advice."

Buffy: "Okay, okay. So stop kibitzing and turn the page already."

There's just no news in newspapers these days. No wonder they use them to make cat litter.

Excuse me.
Cat coming through here....

The only way to control my diet is to shop for it myself.

Quit horsing around. Are you wearing blinkers or something?
Of course I'm Cinderella's handsome prince. Now let's go!

've tried saying "giddy-up" several times but he just keeps going up and down. Perhaps I should dangle a carrot in front of him.

There are so many "isms" in modern art—cubism, futurism, expressionism, and surrealism. I'd like to think I've captured them all in my self portrait.

The name is Bond. James Bond. FYI, my
milk doesn't need to be shaken or stirred.

I'll only sign for it if you promise it's not a reminder to visit the vet's office.

Hey, Doc. Don't even think about it!

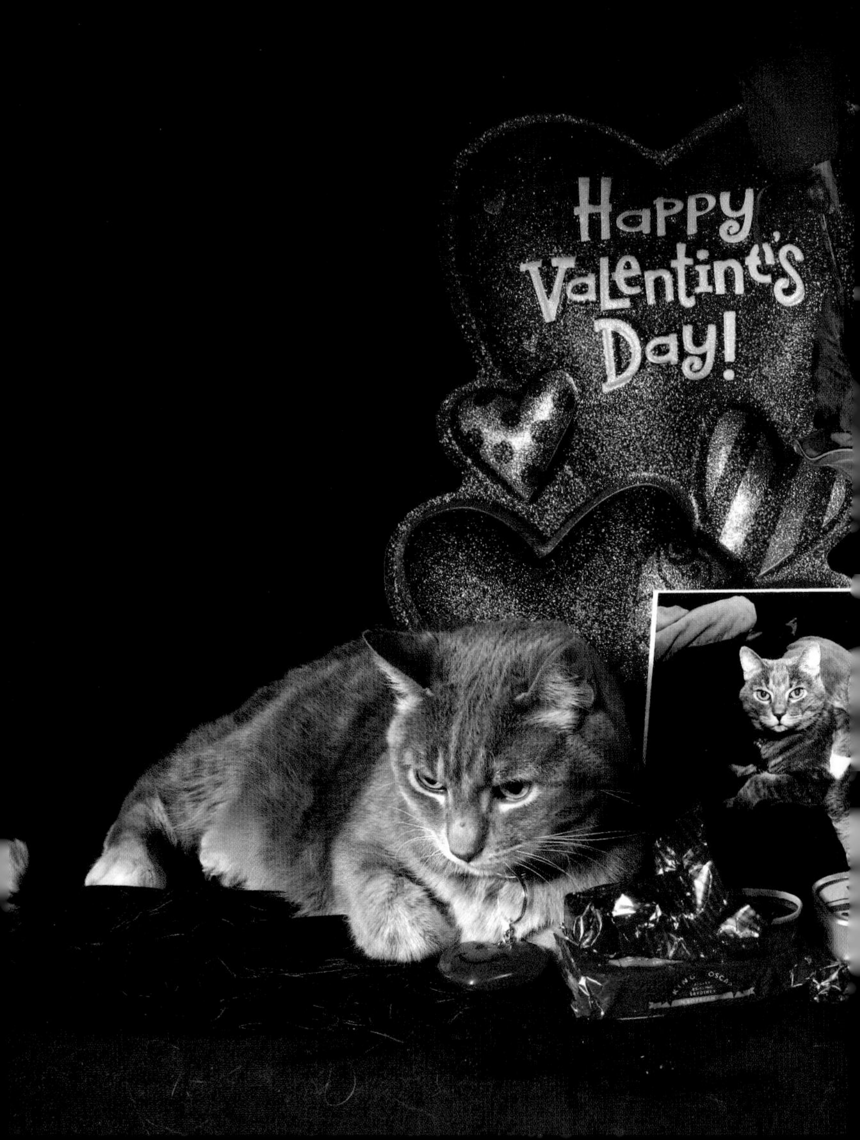
Happy Valentine's Day!

If love is in the air,
it smells like sardines.

What's with the horseradish all over my Passover gefilte fish? Bring on the chopped liver already!

Okay, okay. I'll say it. *Olé.*

Happy now? But truthfully, I can't really enthuse over salsa and chips.

Hey, Uncle Sam.
I'm ready for the
Fourth of July.

So what have we got here? Oooh goody! My favorite freeze-fried chicken treats and those yummy tuna flakes.

That stash was a really good start to Halloween. On to the next house. Riddle me this, riddle me that. Who's afraid of a ginger bat-cat?

It may be Thanksgiving,
but this looks too good to share.

Happy New Year.
Is this the Year of the Cat?

Oh dear.
Another
New Year's
resolution
down the
drain.

Call it a hidden talent. My nails make a really great plectrum for playing lead guitar.

YES! Feline groovy....

It's my turn to hog the remote. Hopefully there's a good game of tennis to watch. I love keeping an eye on the ball.

Just checking that
the coast is clear.

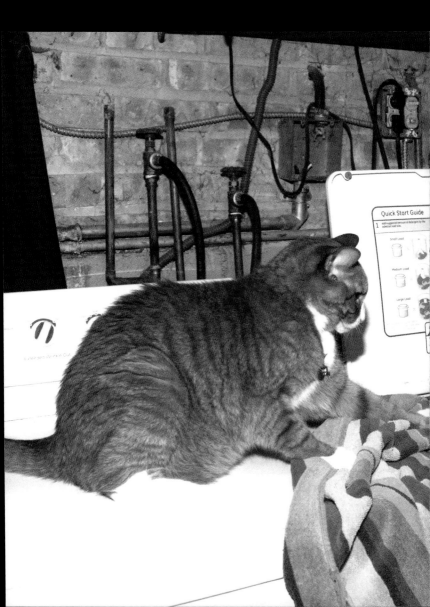

Quick Start Guide

1. Add suggested amount of detergent for the selected wash size.

Small Load

Medium Load

Large Load

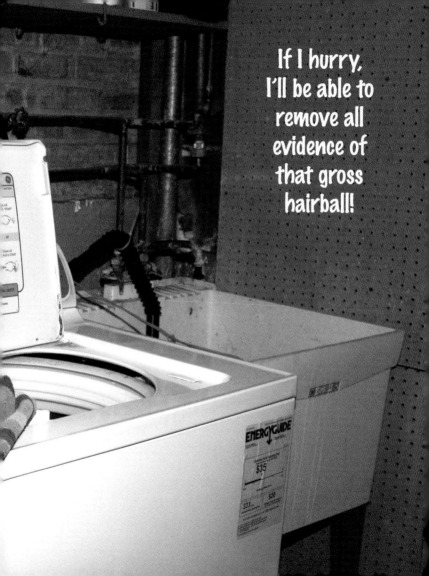